Commissioned by the American Guild of Organists
for the Biennial National Convention
Atlanta, Georgia, June - July 1992

With funding provided by Carl and Sally Gable
In honor of Sarah L. Martin

VOYAGE

a fantasy for organ

by

Dan Locklair

e.c. kerby ltd.

Distributed by

Hal Leonard Publishing Corporation

7777 West Bluemound Road   P.O. Box 13819   Milwaukee, Wisconsin 53213

VOYAGE
a fantasy for organ
by
Dan Locklair

VOYAGE was commissioned by the American Guild of Organists for its 1992 Biennial National Convention in Atlanta, Georgia. Funding for the commission was supplied by Carl and Sally Gable in honor of Sarah L. Martin in recognition of her unique leadership in the study of organ within the Atlanta area.

Sarah Martin, a former Dean of the Atlanta AGO Chapter and General Chairman of the 1992 Biennial National Convention, is an Instructor of Organ in the School of Music at Georgia State University. She also serves as Organist and Music Associate at Druid Hills Baptist Church. According to former student, Sally Gable, as musician and leader, Sarah Martin has gained the respect, admiration and love of her colleagues and of all who have had the privilege of being inspired and motivated by her teaching.

****

VOYAGE, though in four sections, is played in one movement without pause.

Though adaptable to any size organ, it was conceived for a large instrument and manual suggestions indicate this conception:

I	=	Choir
II	=	Great
III	=	Swell
IV	=	Antiphonal
V	=	Bombarde

Section III may utilize chimes, if available. The notation in this section is somewhat unconventional :

$\circ$ / $\flat$. = Free meter, with half note being the unit of beat.

♮ = Usually a pedal note of long, unmeasured value. Hold each pitch until it moves to the next note.

ρ⌒ = Sustained note. Indicated at the notehead, pitches so indicated should be held until a release is indicated either by a ♪ (for specific pitch) or by a ˒ for the release of multiple, held pitches.

All other note values and rests are proportional to the half note.

Accidentals apply for the duration of each system of music.

Total duration of **VOYAGE** : ca. 15' 30"

August, 1991
Winston-Salem, North Carolina

VOYAGE

I.

Dan Locklair

*If an antiphonal division does not exist, this fanfare section (ms. 1-69) should either be played on alternating reeds of separate divisions or the entire section played on one manual (color).

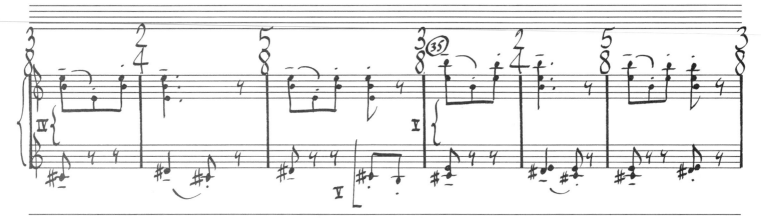

(4)

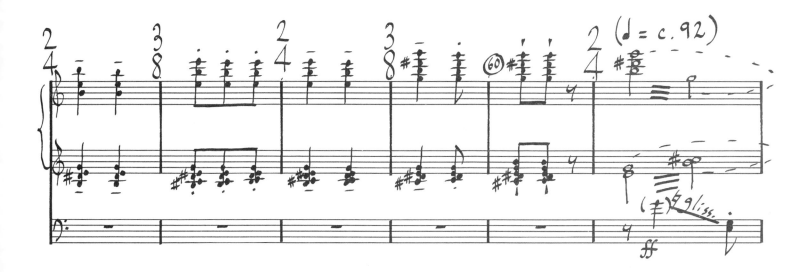

(With a sense of
both the curious
and the bizarre)

(6)

(8)

* See page 2 for notation explanation. Though free of regular, metric accents, all note values and rests are in proportion to the half note. Attention is especially called to the distinction between the half rest (▬ = one pulse) and the whole rest (▬ = two pulses).

C—14 R

(Flute 4' with chimes)

Celeste
strings
(III)

Diapason 4'
(or Flute 4') on
antiphonal division
if available

(18)

(19)

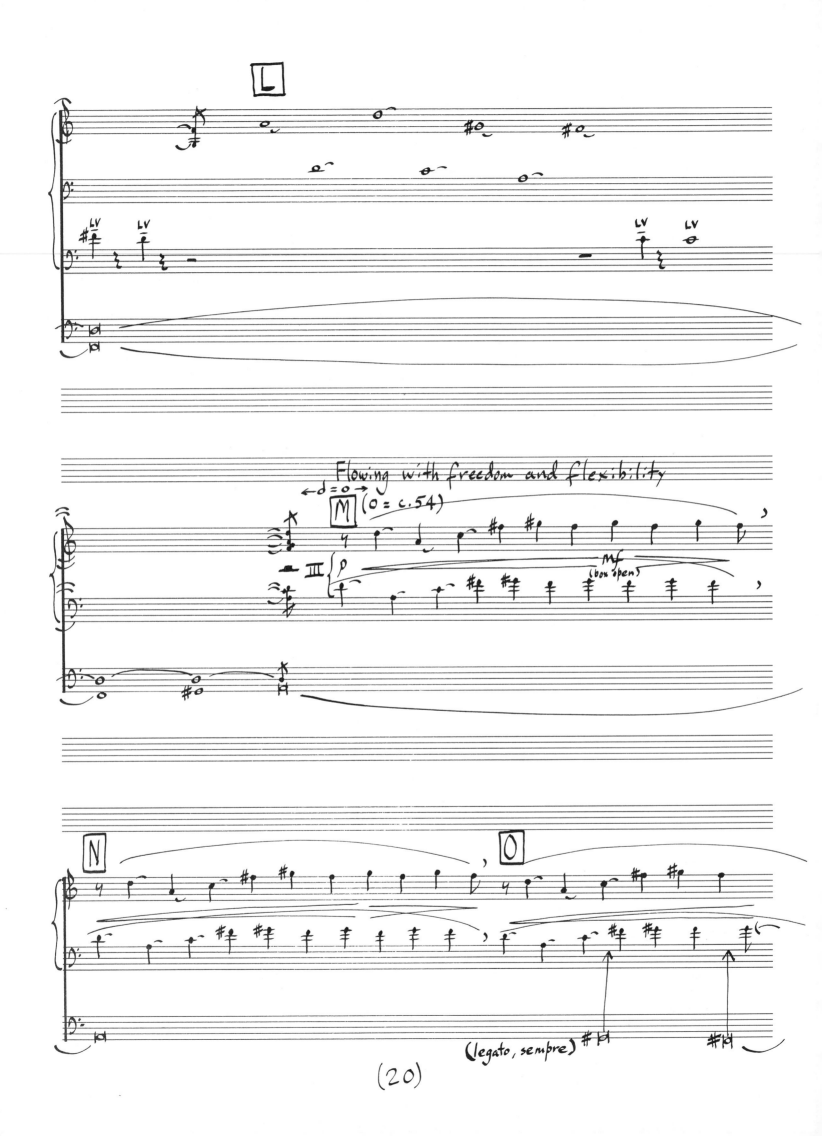

(20)

(21)

Gradually begin to move tempo ahead
205
(add)
(mp)
(gradually increase registration and dynamics)
(add)
(mp)
(d = c. 69)
(Becoming more and more excited)
210
II
(mf)
(Manuals coupled)
mf
(as with manuals, gradually build)
(Foundations 16', 8', manuals coupled)
(d = c. 84)
215
(f)
(add)
(f)

*The performer may remain on II or switch manuals in similar passages of this section of the piece. Also, in similar passages as (237), the pedal may be increased.

(28)

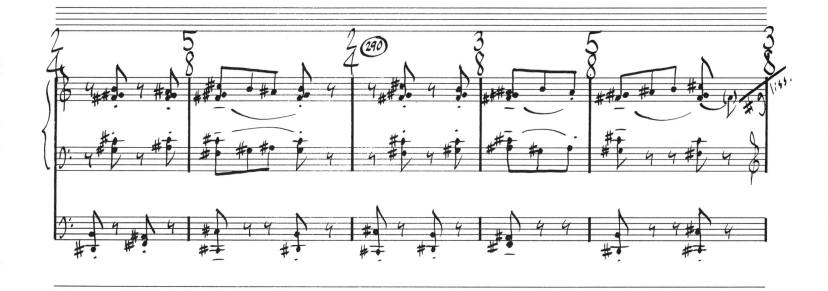

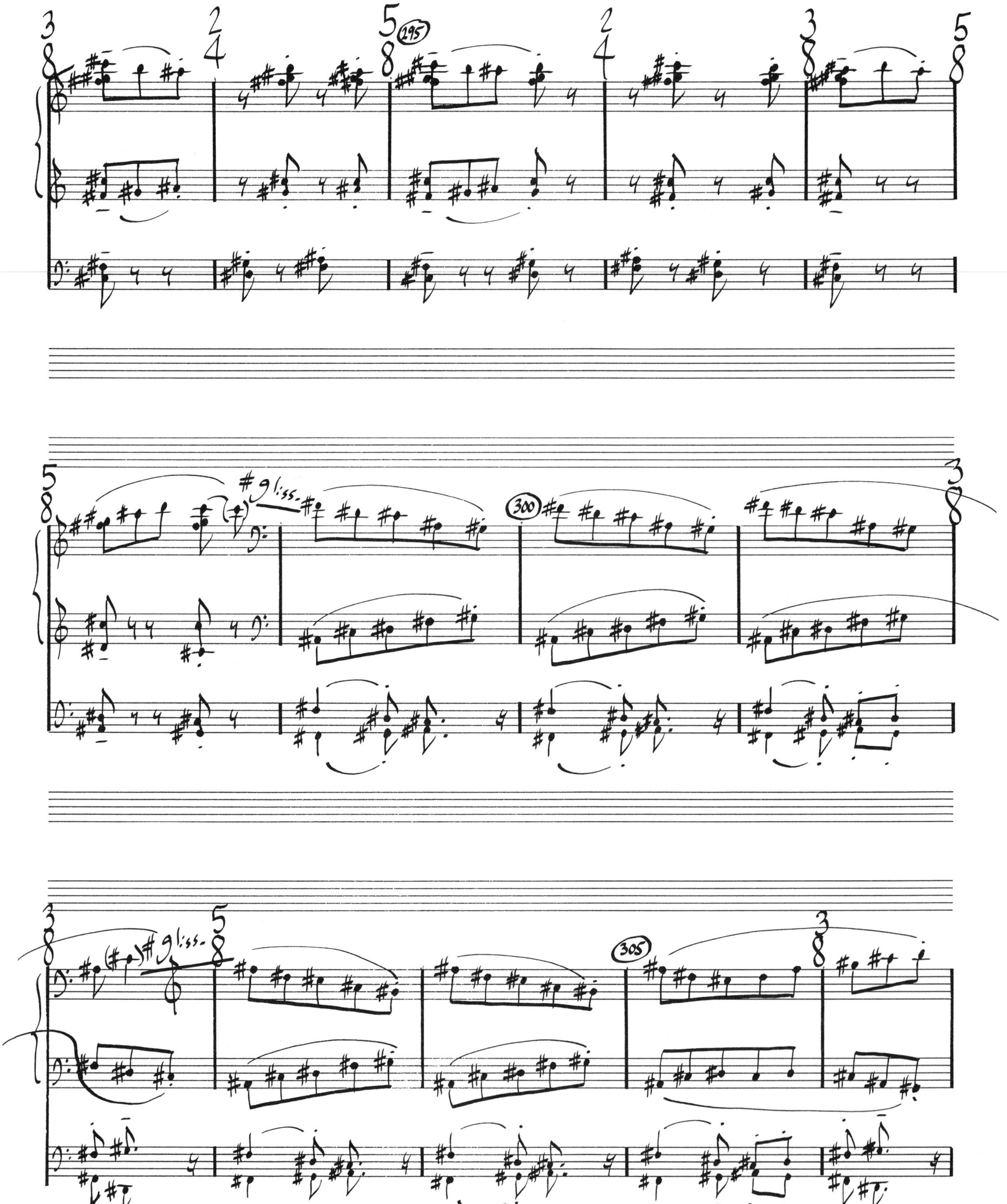
295
gliss.
300
gliss.
305

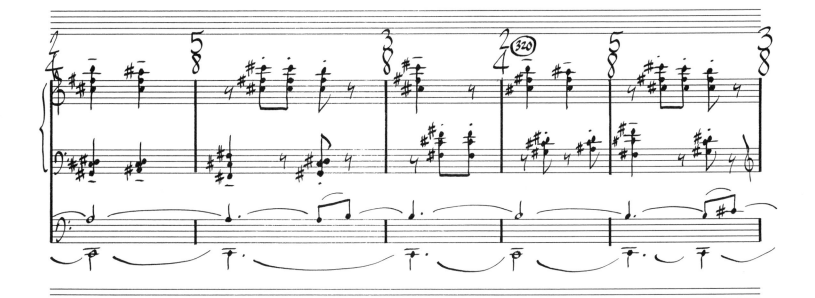

(34)

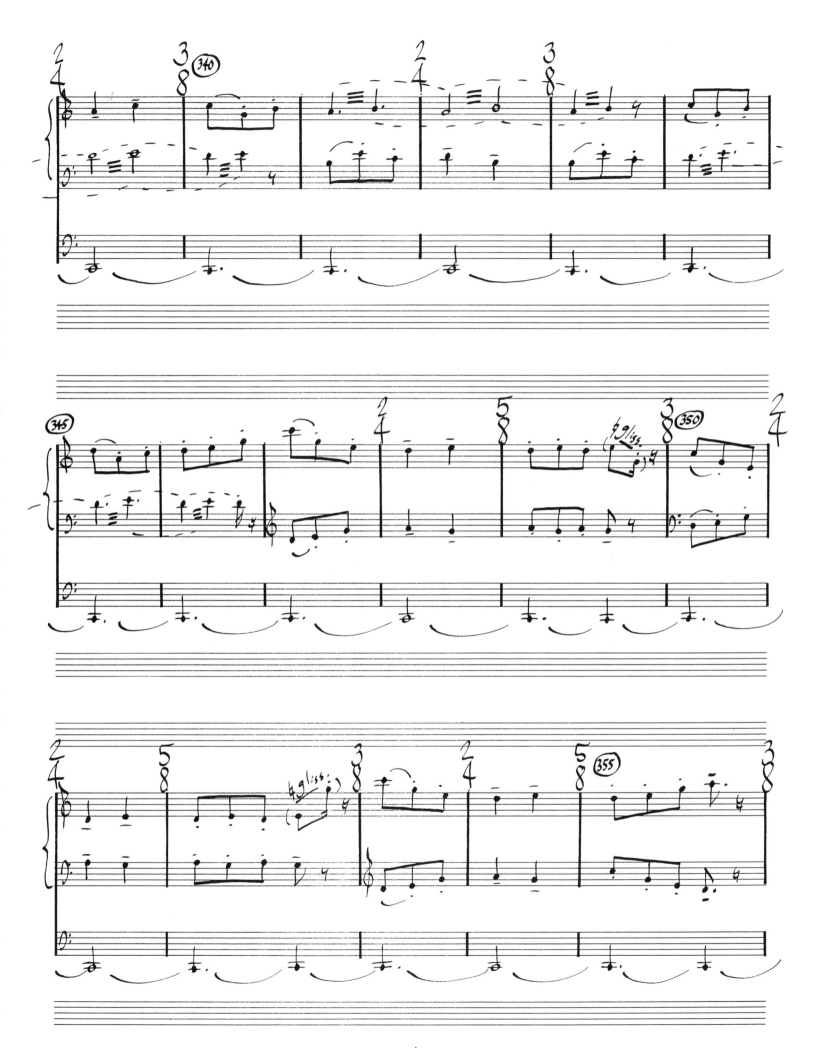

390 Ad lib. tempo
Dramatic!
#gliss.
Exhilarating and quick (♩. = c. 108 or ♩ = c. 162)
legato
II (off antiphonal division)
legato
legato sempre
395
gliss.
400
gliss.

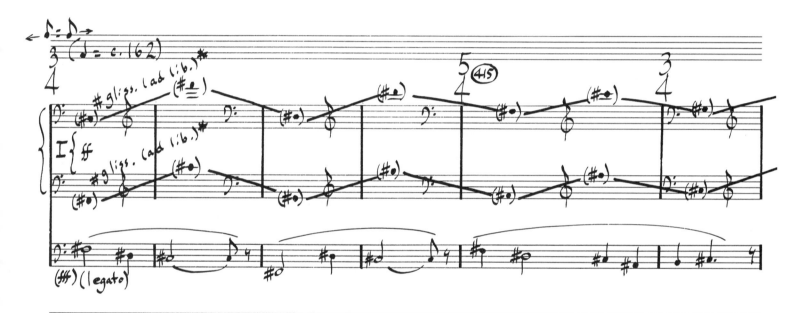

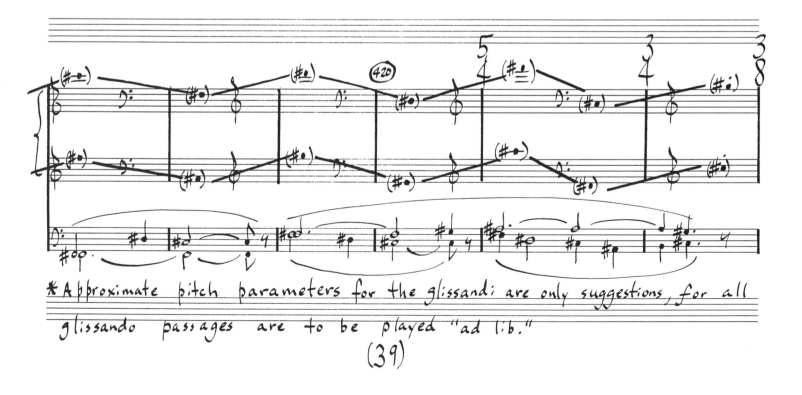

*A pproximate pitch parameters for the glissandi are only suggestions, for all glissando passages are to be played "ad lib."

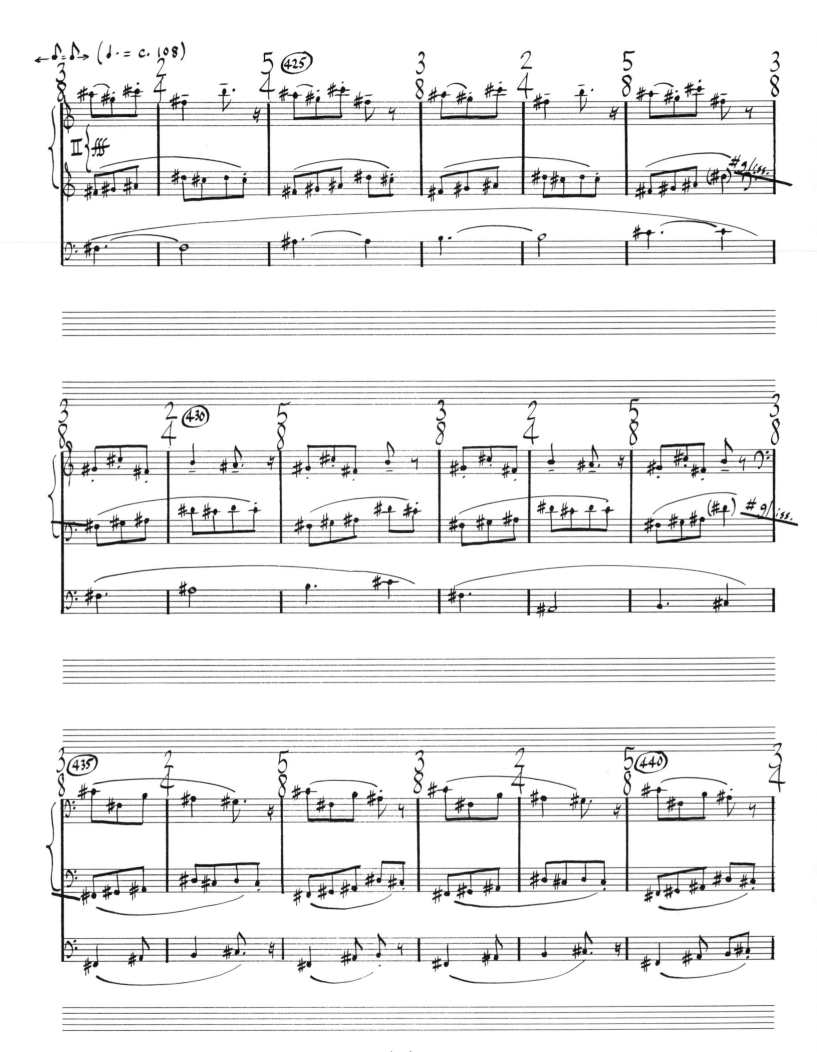

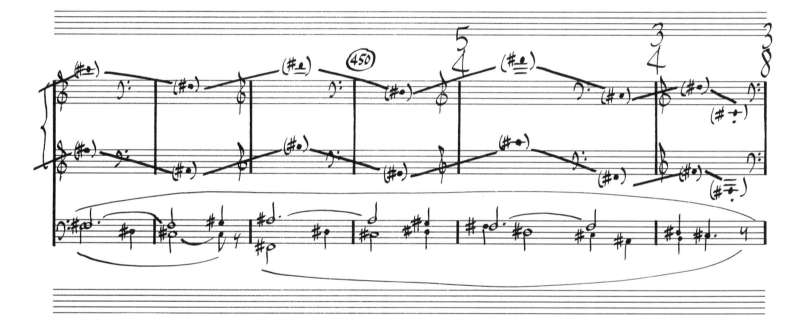

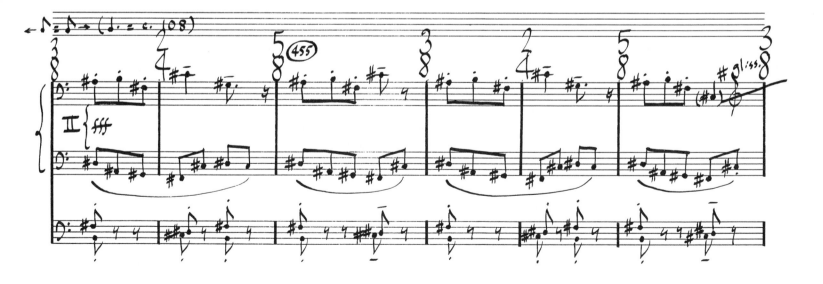

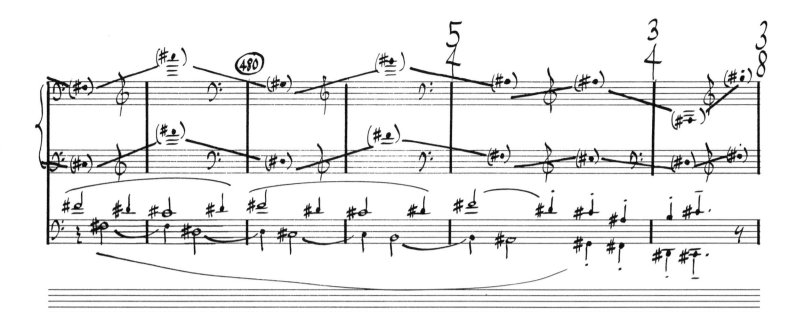

Exultant

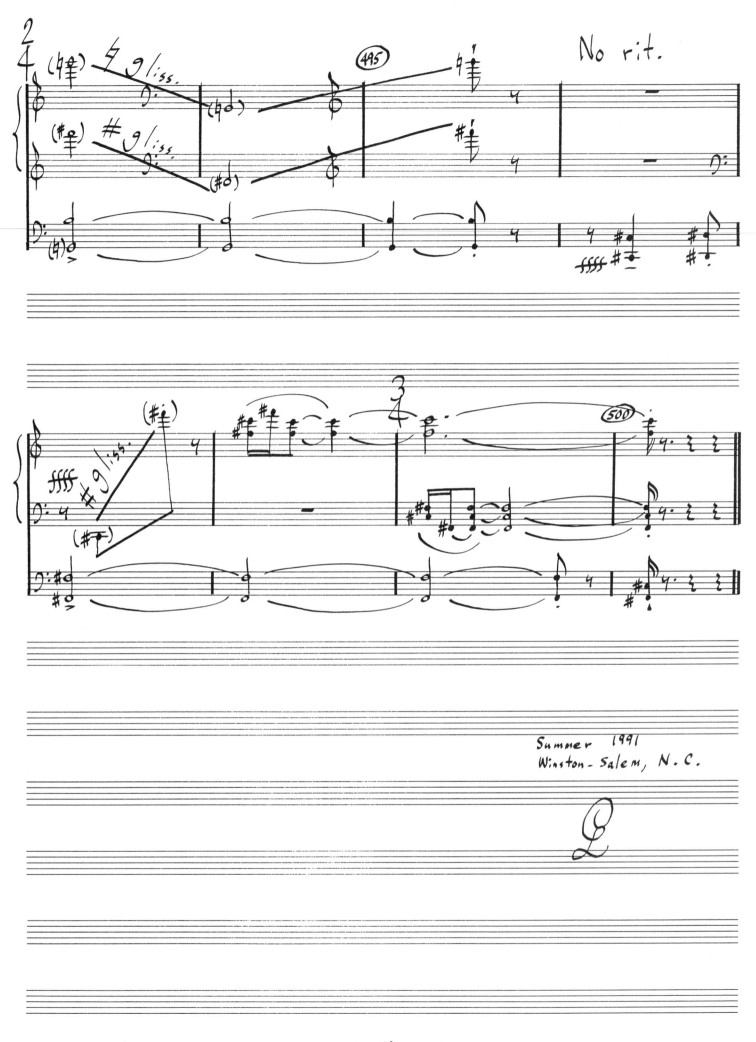

No rit.

Summer 1991
Winston-Salem, N.C.

(44)